# DEDICATION

This book is for Ali and James, Ryan and Keita, Tom and Laura, Matt and Emma.

We hope it's published in time for you to use some of the advice. If it's not, it'll make a brilliant wedding gift for one of your friends, so buy them one and we'll sign it. In fact, buy them one each and we'll sign them both.

# INTRODUCTION

You know how cookbooks are just a starting point for baking? Or how pavements are suggestions as to where you might walk? Well this book is not a rule book for how you should plan a wedding. Rather, this book is simply a series of prompts to get you thinking about marriage and how to enjoy, yes enjoy the process of preparing for it. If you follow even a few of the simple tips and thought teasers in this book, you may just end up as happy as our friend Griff:

*Griff is a cat and he is happy because he hasn't been sucked in to following ridiculous social norms and really doesn't give two hoots about conforming. Who says you've got to sit on a chair with your bottom?*

# WHERE TO FIND THE WISDOM

# IT IS NOT ABOUT "THE BIG DAY"

Surprisingly for me, I had it all planned out. Kara and I would drive from our home in Bournemouth, all the way into the Brecon Beacons in Wales where we would swim in a pool under a waterfall. I would then pretend to see something at the bottom of the pool, dive down to it and emerge, god-like, with an engagement ring in hand, and propose to her there and then. Unbeknownst to me however, it was the first day of the school holidays, so the traffic was just horrendous, made even more so by the torrential rain. As we arrived in Brecon four hours behind schedule, and the sun burst through the leaden sky, I was briefly buoyed, thinking it's going to work out. Instead, at that very moment, my tyre burst, my front suspension collapsed and my wonderful van gave up the ghost right there and then on the side of the road. As Bully the Mercedes Vito crumbled into an unrecoverable mess, my plans fell apart right before my eyes, Kara was there – with a beaming smile, helping me to figure out what on earth we did next. Laughing with friendly passers-by and giving me the support I very much needed right then, I decided that I would still propose to her that evening - if we could still be smiling after what could only be described as a fairly catastrophic few hours, then she was definitely the girl for me.

Luckily for me, she said yes, and like some sort of symbolic closing of my bachelor days, we drove Bully to the scrapyard, adorned him with flowers and left him to start our new chapter together.

Once all the excitement of telling friends and relatives had died down, little did I know what fun lay ahead of us in the form of 'Wedding Administration' or 'Wedmin' as it is now known.

This book is the book I wish I read after that moment - a short friendly guide to prepare those to be married, for what is about to come.

Written for you, it contains all the lessons we learnt through the process of planning our wedding and the things that we realised could have been done differently, or better, or in fact, not been done at all.

"Erm, why should we listen to you? You're not wedding planners!" we hear you cry.

That's a very valid point. You shouldn't. That's why some of the advice you'll receive is from other people we've spoken to. Friends, family, siblings, suppliers and Sod's law have all taught us lessons that we've built into this book.

If you listen to at least some of it, there's a likelihood that you'll soon be saving yourself some pennies and a whole load of heartache and faff (the perfect execution of utterly pointless tasks that get you nowhere).

We'll share many of our small insights throughout, but probably one of our biggest realisations was pretty profound.

It's not about 'THE BIG DAY'.

Ok, wedding planning is of course about the big day BUT it's also an awesome way to get to know each other in new ways, go on mini-adventures and put simply, have loads of fun in becoming a stronger and more effective team who will rock the sh*t out of life.

Don't focus so hard on the end point (which remember is only *ONE* day) that you forget that the planning bit can be fun too.

With this shift in focus, your wedding, the 'big day', becomes one epic arrival ceremony. Yes, you're getting married, but if you have read this book and followed just some of our advice, all your friends and family will basically be welcoming you back from an epic journey of discovery and experimentation.

Throughout this book, you'll find stories and insights interspersed with some exercises for you to do together. Maybe you'll do one, maybe you'll do all, but if there's anything you must do, it is think about the foundations you lay from the outset. When it comes to building things, 80% of the costs and effort will be determined by decisions made early on – this book is here to make sure you nail 'em!

Please note!

This book has been a real collaborative effort, where most chapters are written from both of us to you. Some chapters come from one of us alone and when that happens, we give you the heads up ☺.

# YOUR WEDDING IS MORE THAN JUST A "TO DO LIST

It never is.

It's a list of opportunities to discover something new - whether it's learning a new skill, meeting a new person, or trying a new cuisine.

As soon as you realise this, Wedmin is no longer a chore.

# UMPTIONS

Any kind of book like this must make certain assumptions about the reader. It helps us, the authors, to make sure we write stuff that is useful.

For your information, these are the assumptions we've made about you.

- ✓ One or both of you proposed
- ✓ One of you did the mental calculations and said yes
- ✓ You both still want to get married
- ✓ You're not getting married tomorrow
- ✓ You're not handing over a wad of cash to someone and saying "sort it out and we'll see you on the day".
- ✓ You're not entirely sure on how to start thinking about and / or planning your wedding and need some friendly advice.

# WHY ARE YOU GETTING MARRIED?

Once the excitement of your engagement has calmed down and you start having discussions about the big day, it's important that together you lay some foundations. These are core principles that will help you navigate the road ahead and even help you make some smart decisions as you go.

These foundations are based on one simple question, which when asked, can really make you stop and take stock for a moment. Why are you getting married?

Answering this very simple question should allow you to put things into perspective right from the outset and make sure that whatever you decide to do for your big day, you're doing it for the right reasons.

To get you started, here's an exercise.

## Exercise: Why?
For this exercise you will need:

A cup / glass of your favourite refreshment

A quiet nook at home or in your favourite bolt hole

A note pad and pen

**Time required:**

20mins

**Instructions:**

## Part A

Together, grab your notebooks and pens and each of you retire to your bolt hole. Then, once comfortable, answer the following questions separately:

   1. What does marriage mean to you?

   2. Why do you want to get married to your partner?

## Part B

Once you're both done with Part A, take turns to share your notes. When you're listening to your partner, listen actively, taking notes under the following headings:

   1. What I loved about what you said:

   2. What surprised me about what you said:

After each of you have shared your answers, give your own reflections on what the other has said (using the headings above). If there are some differences or tensions in what you've uncovered, ask about it, discuss and take this opportunity to get to know your partner for life that little bit better.

### Why do this exercise?

There are no right or wrong answers, but before you both run away with organising a huge wedding, it's important to remind yourselves of your true motivations for getting wed. If at the end of this either of you only have "amazing Insta shots"; "get smashed"; "wear that phenomenal Boss Suit / designer dress" as answers, you may wish to have another go – dig deep!

# KNOW WHO YOU ARE ~~MARRYING~~ WORKING WITH

You're a team and awesome teams aren't just formed by awesome individuals but by team members who know how to bring the best out in one another. You've got a project to get over the line together. TOGETHER.

So, you need to figure out how you and your partner like to approach tasks and challenges. You could just have this conversation straight off, but it can be useful to have something to spring from – a conversation starter.

### Who are you and what makes you tick?

As part of your day job, you may very well have come across personality tests as a useful tool for building teams that work.

Ever tried doing one with your partner?

It's surprisingly enlightening and highly recommended!

Why? It is easy to think that because you've spent X amount of years with someone you know them inside out, right? But we aren't all trained psychologists and when forming a premier league Wedmin team, it helps knowing what you're both good at…. and what you kind of suck at.

For example, if your partner is not a completer-finisher but a phenomenal negotiator, you can harness this knowledge and take the lead on getting jobs over the line but let them take the lead on any contract / cost chat. Uncovering these hidden depths will not only help you understand yourself better, it will also allow you as a partnership to capitalise on your strengths and counter your weaknesses and ultimately become a more harmonious Wedmin team! ☺

# Exercise: Get on the couch

## To prepare:

Get online and search for 'Free Myers Briggs Test' – there are lots of free sites that offer it, so choose one and share the link with each other.

## Time required:

30min (test) 30min (sharing)

## Taking the test:

1. Individually, complete the online personality test

2. Based on your responses the test will make some inferences on things like how you like to work and how you make decisions – all important things for your partner to know.

3. Print out the results and share them with your partner **in person**.

## Time to Learn: Sharing results

Listen to your partner, make notes and give feedback utilising the following headings:

1. What surprised you

2. What you recognised / agree with

3. What you think you need to be more mindful of when working together

## Why do this exercise?

These tests will help you both understand how you behave when you are at your best, how you behave when you are stressed or under pressure, and your individual needs, motives and preferences. Being mindful of each other's traits in these situations will be as useful in 10 years' time as it will be now. It will help you understand why your partner might be reacting in a particular way, help you find ways to support one another or perhaps most importantly, help you identify those situations where you may be better off giving them some space to let them work it out for themselves.

*"I think I got somethin' in my teeth, could you get it out for me?*

*That's f\*cking teamwork".*

— Tenacious D.

*"You never really understand a person until you consider things from his point of view... Until you climb inside of his skin and walk around in it."*

— Harper Lee (To Kill a Mockingbird)

# CREATING A SHARED VISION FOR YOUR WEDDING

It is far too easy to dive straight on into the white cloud of wedding bliss that is Pinterest / wedding magazines / Instagram / wedding fayres, before understanding or even thinking about what each of you want from the big day. What starts out as a few innocent bookings for venue viewings (just 'scoping' out options) can soon escalate into:
"Right, crikey, better get a band before all the best ones go. Oh, and caterers - they get booked up quick, not to mention…"

WOOOOOAAAAHHH THERE COWBOY‼

Let's get a bit of calm back in this slightly panic-fuelled, task list-driven wedding rodeo, take a deep breath, and straighten our saddle bags.

Right. Listen up. There are all sorts of big decisions coming your way that are going to seriously smash the team kitty and yes, if you don't agree with your partner when they are pushing for decisions it may seem easier to avoid difficult conversations, telling yourself:
"Well it's what they want and I don't hate it so" …

...but when you are making it rain £50s, in the company of some guests you don't even know the name of, tapping your feet to music you loathe, in a venue that doesn't mean all that much to you, you may just wonder "should I have said something?"

Here's a little exercise to get you talking about what you *both* want from the wedding...

# EXERCISE: BACK TO THE FUTURE PART WEDDING

To get you talking about the serious stuff, this exercise shifts the focus away from material items and gets you both to settle into your newly married shoes.

Comfy?

Now to start developing an understanding of what would truly give you both a big, fat, "so glad we did that" grin – give this a crack.

## What you'll need

1. Four pieces of paper (two each)
2. A pen
3. Your imagination

# Instructions

1. Split each piece into four sections and write at the top of each section one of the following words:
   - A. Thinking
   - B. Feeling
   - C. Saying
   - D. Doing

| Thinking | Feeling |
|---|---|
| Saying | Doing |

2. Now, imagine you have had your wedding (you may even be on your honeymoon) and it was the most outrageously awesome day you could have ever imagined. Write out answers for each of the above (i.e. What are you thinking about it? How are you feeling about it? What are you saying to each other about the ceremony? What do you imagine are you doing? Are you enjoying breakfast with each other with no-one else around, or are you welcoming guests around for some tea and cake?)

3. Once you're done (10-15minutes will do), share your thoughts with one another, actively listening to what the other has to say, taking notes if you like.

By putting yourself in your partner's shoes, you're exercising your empathy muscle – you are practising seeing the world through their eyes. Listen to your partner and get an understanding of their view of the world. Be patient and resist the urge to jump in.

4. After you've heard from each other, get one more piece of paper and do a MoSCoW together. Feel free to make yourselves a Mule to get you by (Recipe in the Annex).

Our Wedding...

# Must...
# Should...
# Could...
# Won't...

These four things now represent your key principles - refer back to them as you go and check in with each other now and again to ensure you're still staying true to your future selves.

For example: "The day afterwards, I want to be feeling like I spoke to everyone, that everyone felt like they were part of the day, that we were generous with our time with them". This might then lead to: "Our wedding must allow us to spend quality time with people.

*Stick to your key principles and you'll be in good stead when the wedding avalanche comes*

# RULES OF ENGAGEMENT
## by Kara
### (With comments from Will)

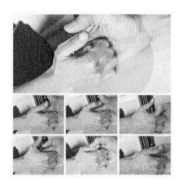

*The brutal game of 'Thumb War' would not be possible without rules to which competitors must abide. The move executed in the above sequence is known as 'the inverted Made You Look" to those in the know.*

Even as someone who turned out to be a touch on the Wedmin-obsessed side, I would happily admit the following: you will need a break! Both of you!

It can be bloody exhausting organising the biggest party of your life - why do you think we left party planning to our parents when we were kids?

I can't remember once having the slightest inclination to want to make my own party bags or organise who got my cake and if you were caught up in worrying about who would like your 'favours' back then, save your precious time now little Timmy. No one gives two measly farts whether you hand-tied those love heart sweets into mini hessian bags.

BUT - you can't be dodging the facts: there is a surprisingly large amount of Wedmin to be done. A whole heap more than you probably first imagined. So how do we strike the balance?

Two Plans of Action (POAs) coming at you:

## Wedmin Timeboxing

You can't be doing Wedmin all the time. Assure the Mr/Mrs that yes, you are still utterly fizzing to decide where you put crazy aunty Julie on the seating plan but just like your phenomenal performances in the bedroom, a little break in play is essential in maintaining your Olympic-standard form. So agree on and allocate some allotted times in the diary that you will block out (Time boxes) and commit to doing your Wedmin tasks then (e.g. 1-2 days per week; 1-2 weekends per month). It may seem dull, but it is necessary, so pour the fiancé a cup of coffee or a G&T, light a candle, whip your diaries out and get compromising.

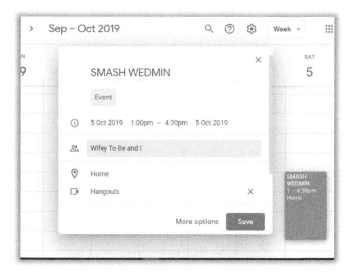

## The 'To Do' List

Having a professional faffer as a husband (*Will: Erm, a bit harsh - I faff for free*) the shared 'To Do' list was a big win. We opted for a roll of easy stick 'whiteboard' paper and put it up on the living room wall. By its prominent place in our living space, it brought a certain sense of comfort in that we were both being held accountable to tasks. At the start of our allocated Wedmin timebox, we would write a list of the most time-sensitive/currently pressing tasks (no more than 10), assign one of our names to it and feel a sense of calm ensue as we steadily put a tick next to each (*Will: I would generally immediately seek praise for any task completed*).

### Exercise: The timeboxed 'To Do' list

To make the seemingly never-ending list of Wedmin tasks that little less daunting, you can have several To Do lists written up at once that need to be addressed at different time points in the wedding planning journey.
YOU DON'T HAVE TO DO IT ALL AT ONCE!

Examples of top row time boxes you may wish to use include: 12 months, 9 months, 3 months, 1 month, week before, day before, the big day, the day after.

For the tech savvy, there are also plenty of digital tools for managing To Do lists out there that you can access when on the move. Trello (www.trello.com) is just one. At the time of writing (May 2019) they have even created a wedding planning template for you to use.

Note: You may find it easier to only have one To Do list up on the wall at any one time and keep this to current priorities only. Remember, we are here for a good time AND a long time. Consider taking down the "To Do" list during Wedmin-free time if you are at home too - otherwise, it just feels like it's always lurking in the background and you'll never be able to forget about it!

"Can we have a detailed to-do list please?" you ask. Everyone is different, so the tasks we had to complete will be different to yours, but the likelihood is that there will be some commonality. There are plenty of wedding websites that will give you an exhaustive list of things you need to do, so we'll not go into the weeds here.

However, we cannot emphasise this enough... please please please, before diving into these granular lists, do the big thinking first. Go through the exercises given in this book in the prior chapters - it will ensure that when you read these lists from pro wedding planners, you can put your own filter on them and identify the tasks that are only relevant to you. They also all assume that you've over 12 months to plan - this might not work for you and you'll need to cut your plans according to your cloth of time and money.

| DATE / TASK | 9 Months | 3 Months | 1 Month | Day Before | On The Day | The Day After |
|---|---|---|---|---|---|---|
| GUEST COMMS | SEND INVITES | CHASE UP RSVPS | | Brief MC | Leave it to the MC | |
| ENTERTAINMENT | Confirm Band Delegate to team | | Start Playlist Collection | Install PA Sound Check | | |
| CATERING | Find caterers to try out | Confirm Caterer | Confirm details | Confirm details | Enjoy | Scoff Leftovers Give cake to mates |
| AND SO ON... | | | | | | |

# HOW TO FIND TIME

Whilst creating time boxes to do Wedmin is brilliant, you'd be surprised what you can do in what would otherwise be 'dead' time. Half of Wedmin is just making decisions according to the info you've got, so if you're both together, twiddling your thumbs, put that time to good use and nail some tasks. If one of you is not in the mood, be honest – but don't forget to be kind when you do so. For example "I'm really enjoying this radio documentary about the mating rituals of the Mayfly. Can we save it for our Wedmin day tomorrow please?"

Some of you, like Kara, may be particularly good at spotting these opportunities to get sh*t done.

"I found long car journeys best. There was nothing quite like letting the hubby-to-be settle himself into an episode of desert island discs before, *BAM!* - radio off – Wedmin to address – answers required – no escape.

In my defence, I did always pack snacks".

# YOUR PRIORITIES MAY HAVE TO CHANGE

Depending on each of your approaches to Wedmin, you may find that getting those ticks on the To Do list tends to be more of a priority to your other half than you, or vice versa.

What this means is that when one partner chases the other about something they said they would do but haven't, it comes across as nagging. This sucks for both parties.

So, the key bit here is that if you or your other half have promised to do something, **do it**.

A natural reaction to such a statement might be: "yeah, ok, but I've got swimming, coffee dates, work, gym ......" all legitimate reasons. But not enough to renege on your promise.

If you care about what makes a happy partner, then their priorities will begin to merge with yours. Better than this, when you stick to your promises it shows your partner that you take their concerns seriously, leaving them with a warm fuzzy feeling of being listened to and valued.

But we know that all good relationships must involve a bit of give AND take (i.e. they need to also recognise what is most important to you too) so after a few evenings of hand painting mini sailing boats as favours (true story), if you're marrying someone human, they should recognise that a little you/gym/shed/swim/chill time is well deserved.

# WHEN THINGS GO TITS UP

The gritty truth of Wedmin: at some point, sh*t will hit the proverbial fan. People *may* screw up, some people *may* try and make a fast buck at your expense, and sure, your marquee *may* get gale-force blown and torn to pieces the day before your wedding.
Sucks right?

WRONG!

This is your time to *learn* Young Padawans!

Just like travelling with your partner when one of you has a bad case of Bali belly, you will see your partner at their worst but you will also learn a whole heap about each other in the process, developing an understanding of how they think and how they cope with life's little curveballs. This is one of the reasons why we learnt to love Wedmin - gaining insights such as this can be hugely valuable for a lifelong relationship where there will undoubtedly be a fair few more curveballs coming your way!

For Example:

**Kara:** "I wanted to immediately share my stresses and worries with my family and friends"

**Will:** "I would very much rather keep our private woes, well, private".

What we noticed:

We learnt we dealt with things differently and this meant we had to compromise. Will had to learn to feel comfortable letting Kara share our stresses with those close to us, whilst Kara had to learn that maybe telling the bus driver AND the postman about her stress palpitations firmly qualified as oversharing.

The humbling part: when initially thrown to you, these curveballs can suck. But, when they've been swerved or you are in the process of hitting them out of the park, you get treated to a little beautiful reminder of all the people in your life prepared to come right on in and bat for you. And WOW, does it feel good to be part of that team.

Smash those curveballs, talk, laugh and teamwork your way over the obstacles and come out the other side wiser, stronger Jedi than when you started.

# MAKE SHIT!

Us humans are born with all the essentials needed to make things. Yet as soon as we discover an unmet need in our lives, we are straight onto Gumtree, eBay, or Amazon, to find a solution. To buy. To consume. It is such a waste. Not of the stuff that you'll end up throwing away, but of *you*. Of what you are and what you can do. There is nothing more pure or human than making an idea reality. To translate a thought, a feeling, a flash of neuronal activity, into a physical object that EXISTS! That's a privilege we've been granted by Mother Nature that we should be using every single day.

So,

Embracing the Maker in you has a plethora of benefits beyond just saving you money. It can also be an opportunity to:

- Learn a new skill
- Get your creative juices pumping
- Make friends / family feel part of the day by feeling like they've been able to contribute in some way
- Inspire the "makers" in your friends & family, helping them to uncover hidden talents that you, or they, didn't know existed (it turns out our usher Dan had some ridiculous sketching talent tucked away!)
- Work on projects with the other half that get you away from the computer screen
- Put your mark on the day

If you feel awkward asking people to help, here are two suggestions:

1.  Think about how YOU would feel if that person asked you to help with their wedding. If the feeling is positive - there's your answer! You are worrying unnecessarily.

2.  Ask people if they would do it as a wedding gift. Our friend Hollie made our wedding cake which was incredible, saved us loads of dosh and made it feel all the more special on the day knowing it had been slaved over by someone who truly cared about us (she offered to make it when a little merry and she still wanted to when sober - win!).

# MAKER TOP TIPS

## Top Tip 1:
### Use free/recycled materials where possible

It saves money, saves the earth and gives you a ridiculous amount of satisfaction after the wedding when you can throw it in the recycling without seeing pound signs disappearing before your very eyes. Even better - you may be able to qualm-free pass it on to another bride and groom knowing you've saved them money (great mate) and saved space in the shed (even better).

## Top Tip 2:

### "Steal like an Artist", *Austin Kleon*

As Tyler Durden says in his Fight Club soliloquy, you are not a unique snowflake. Whilst we don't 100% agree, he has a point. Likelihood is that whilst you may be endeavouring to be original, your vision for your big day is just a twist on something you've seen before. Don't tip toe around this, embrace it. Outrageously consume ideas from everywhere – nature, the Mardi Gras, funerals, gigs and festivals – they're all sources of inspiration in one way or another. Learning to steal with pride is a skill that will continue to benefit you for the rest of your life.

## Top Tip 3:

### Upskill

Once you know what you want to build or create, the likelihood is that someone has figured out how to do it.

So have a little look on Instructables, YouTube, or even better, ask someone who can teach you/knows someone that may be willing to share their knowledge and skills.

Don't know how to build that Steam Punk wedding arch? Learn to Weld.
Want to make your own Cravat? Learn to sew.
Is there ever going to be a better excuse to learn a new skill, if not to make something special for your wedding day?

"GOOD ARTISTS COPY.

GREAT ARTISTS STEAL."

-    Pablo Picasso

Top Tip 4:
Weigh up time investment and potential of stress Vs fun/cost saving
Although making stuff is awesome, some things in life really are worth paying for. If it is going to cause you or your partner stress or lots of late nights/lost weekends that could otherwise be spent doing something more inherently fun to you, it may just be that the money is worth investing.

# THE POWER OF COMPROMISE

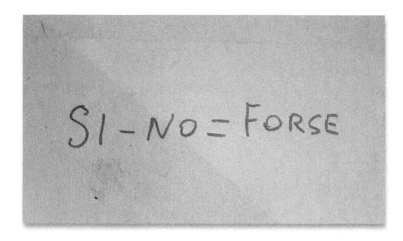

I took this picture of some graffiti when in Italy. I thought it was a statement about how an argument between 'Si' (Yes) and No (No!) can lead to tension – a force for healthy debate. I later learnt that 'Forse' in Italian meant 'Maybe'. I loved this little bit of graffiti a little bit more. I imagine two lovers arguing, when one, with pen in hand and defeated, wrote up with hope in his heart, 'Forse' before they walked away into the night, hand in hand.

The moral of the story? Embrace the disagreements, find the middle ground if it exists and move on. You won't agree on everything, it would be boring if you did.

"Eat a live frog first thing in the morning and nothing worse will happen to you the rest of the day."

– Mark Twain

# SO...
# SWALLOW THE FROG!

For those of you still baffled by the title - this is about kicking our procrastination monkey to the curb. Some of you may be aaaaalll about Wedmin and have absolutely zero issues cracking on and doing the hard stuff. Gold star you kick ass completer - you may progress to the next level.

Still sitting there looking at your frog? Still putting off the difficult tasks, the awkward conversations, the decisions you know you have to make?

Stop using that broom to brush Wedmin under the carpet and get it firmly up your arse!

Here's how:

## Exercise: Timeline Reality Check

- With a wedding still several months away it is easy to feel that you have loads of time left. No sweat. All under control, right?

- In reality, the time within those months that could be dedicated to Wedmin is likely to be a lot less than you think ( i.e. '6 weeks' in a calendar may end up actually only being 8 hours of Wedmin time after accounting for work, sleep, socialising, exercising and any other pulls on your time. That's 1 day! )

- So sit down with your calendar and future life partner and be realistic about when and where there is time for Wedmin.

- Once this is calculated, allocate how much time you are going to dedicate to getting each task done and more importantly, when! Shared calendars (paper or online) really help with this.

- Organising your time like this will save you from booking too many weekends up immediately prior to the wedding and running around manically sorting things out last minute.

Love Birds or Worker Bees?

So when you do try and get something done as a couple, rather than achieving anything, do you stare longingly and unproductively into each other's eyes, distract each other with startling wit and repartee? If yes, then that's lovely – just plan in your Wedmin for when you are flying solo and your lovely but distracting fellow love bird is not around. Bottle up your energies and be a furiously productive little bee in their absence and prepare to stun them with your progress on their return home.

## Exercise: The Backwards To-Do List

This exercise is super simple.
- Write out your current to-do list.
- Now score each task in order of how difficult they are for you to complete.
- You know what's coming
- Now, say the words "Swallow The Frog" and do the most difficult tasks first.

- Once done, give yourselves a massive pat on the back. It will honestly be a weight off your shoulders. All you have to do now is crack on with the tasks you'll enjoy. Or at least, dislike a little less☺.
- Swallow The Frog*. It's surprisingly good for you.

(*NO FROGS WERE HARMED DURING THE MAKING OF THIS BOOK)

---------------------------------------------

NOTES / DOODLES / REFLECTIONS!

# THE ALMIGHTY SEND-OFF

A bit like most things in this book, the gathering of one's nearest and dearest for a stag / hen / bachelor / bachelorette party can take many forms. So rather than pretend we can give you the perfect party on a plate, here are a few nudges to keep things on the right track and not let this 'send-off' of sorts end up with you in a crotch hugging tutu / morphsuit™, smashing back sickly sweet shots on a night out in Benidorm, when all you really craved for was a quiet pint round the campfire with your Dad and your dog (or vice versa!).

## Exercise: The Art of Constraints

We aren't encouraging you to take the organisational reins here (you don't need something else to be planning right now), but equally, it doesn't hurt to give whoever is organising your send off some help. So, when you task them up, think about it as a military operation. On the following pages are some templates for each of you to copy and complete. Once done, organise a sit down with your respective organiser(s) and talk them through it. They may well have a very well-defined idea of what they want to do for you, or they may not have any idea whatsoever. Whichever way, they are likely your best friend, so help them or compromise if needed. Remember, it's a real privilege to have someone do this for you, no matter how it ends up. Embrace it all and thank them for it with open arms.

Examples of 'constraints': Has to be in the UK, has to cost no more than 'X', has to allow parents / older generation to feel involved, got to have at least one good meal. Don't be too demanding - give them freedom and if they screw it up, so what? It'll be another story to tell.

## IT'S ALL ABOUT ME ME ME

If you want to be a bit selfish, do it, particularly when it comes to who is there. If you have to make some tough decisions on who to invite along, say from the outset that it's a super small gathering and manage expectations. People will understand, especially if they're on the right hand side of the age histogram...

# MISSION

OBJECTIVE

LOCATION

BALLPARK COST

ESSENTIAL ATTENDEES

DURATION

DATES

# MISSION

OBJECTIVE

LOCATION

BALLPARK COST

ESSENTIAL ATTENDEES

DURATION

DATES

# NEEEEEEXT!

If you have some older friends and family but are slightly worried about the potential consequences of grandad George taking a paintball to the nuts, fear not! Think about how you could design the send-off so that Georgie boy can come along – could you have a decent dinner at the beginning of the weekend, or hold a more gentile gathering at another time?

One note of caution: be mindful of how much it may be costing others both in time and money – show empathy and let them know that you're cool if they can't make it. There's nothing worse than feeling you're letting someone down, so try and lower the barriers to their participation where you can.

# TAKING CARE OF THE PIGGY BANK

This is undoubtedly the thing that all couples will need to have some proper grown up chats about, combined with and some jolly good sprinkles of compromise during the build up to the wedding day.

## First things first: Set an overall budget

When doing this, a good dose of healthy perspective can be achieved by talking about not what you are prepared to *gain* as a result of spending your money, but what you are prepared to *sacrifice*. You see as humans, we are actually more motivated by minimising risk than we are by maximising gains (yep, proper actual psychology here peeps).

It is known as 'loss aversion' and has been proven in research to be a far more powerful force for leverage than focusing on how you might benefit from any given situation – for us humans it would appear that 'losses loom larger than gains'.

An example of this 'loss aversion' is seen in an experiment by Homonoff (2017) at Cornell University. In her experiment, she wanted to determine which approach had the biggest impact on reducing plastic bag use in Washington D.C. In one region, people were 'taxed' $0.05 for every disposable plastic bag they used at a super market, whilst in the other region, people were given a $0.05 bonus for every reusable bag they used. The results? In the taxed region, usage of disposable bags dropped by 42%. In the 'bonus' region, there was no change in usage. A fascinating example of where people are more willing to change their behaviour in response to the risk of a loss than the prospect of a gain.

Why is this relevant here? Because no matter how frugal you may be, weddings can come with a significant price tag - one which could equate to covering something else fairly significant in one's lifetime. If you think about not what you are spending on your wedding, but what you are choosing not to spend money on instead, you will shift your point of reference and be more inclined not to splurge that extra few hundred on something that brings you little joy.

So what's it to be? Flights to Rome, or 100 bread rolls?

For example:

Expensive wedding (£40K+) = Deposit for a four bed semi-detached house in a coastal town, a short walk from the beach.

Average UK wedding (£20K) = Deposit for a two bed house in Bournemouth and a trip to Italy with some serious pasta eating rolled in.

For those of you interested in saving up a nest egg for your future selves, £20K invested in a mutual / index fund with a return of 7%, will in 30 years' time (when you'll be thinking of retirement perhaps) be worth over £160K. (Read Tony Robbins' super accessible 'Unshakeable' for a real wake-up call on this one).

Discussing what you are prepared to sacrifice for your wedding will help you both be more realistic about the absolute maximum you are happy to spend. Once you've decided, stick to it - it will be way more fun finding fun work-arounds (ways to achieve the same effect but for significantly less money / effort).

With the overall budget agreed, it is now down time to decide how to allocate your money. Again, this will depend on where your priorities lie. Revisit your answers to the prioritisation exercises on this to guide how you allocate funds with cost Vs payoff in mind (i.e. will it honestly make a difference to your enjoyment of the day?).

# SPREADSHEETS – BORING OR SEXY?

You need to manage your spending. Full stop. Create a wedding finance spreadsheet with all foreseeable costs included (anything from your catering to the registrar). Enter in any fixed costs and agree a maximum amount for other items (e.g. no more than £XXX on flowers). Update it as you go and as you talk to suppliers and get quotes,. All the little stuff adds up so try and be as disciplined as you can and track your spending as you go.

There are lots of wonderful people who have built websites and templates that can help you with your budget management, but if you can't find anything that works for you, download a copy of our spreadsheet via our Facebook page to help you create a budget and then keep track of your spending. (Regarding the payment of invoices, your suppliers have to put bread on their own tables too – so be prompt in paying them and be a good customer. There is nothing more likely to sour a relationship than not paying what is due).

# THE GREAT WEDDING CREDIT DECEPTION
## (by Kara)

When staring agape at my friend Kate, having just heard her sister spent over £500 on wedding underwear, she said to me "but that's the thing with weddings, somewhere in our addled brains, money is traded for "wedding credits" and soon you find yourself thinking 'well if the venue was 100 wedding credits and the underwear is like 8 wedding credits then it doesn't seem so bad".

And she had a point.

The point she had was that with money disappearing in all directions, it is easy to normalise spending and get yourself into situations where you are agreeing with your wedding caterer that £1.50 per head for extra bread is perfectly reasonable...

...until you realise that is *before* VAT (always check this) and with over 100 guests that's another £180 for bread.

BREAD!

So how do we save ourselves from the wedding credit trap?

We create a wedding credit *exchange*.

A bit like in the loss aversion idea, seeing £180 still sitting in your account after making a saving is actually not all that rewarding. The likely outcome is that your £180 "who needs bloody bread?" money will get swallowed up in other wedding spends. Allocating that £180 saved to booking a night in the luxury hotel room you've been salivating over feels far more rewarding. Keep your focaccia – I'm getting us a seaside bungalow and a big sexy cocktail!

50

So, before your Wedmin gets into full swing, think about those other non-wedding things that you could be saving towards. You can do this manually on post-its, a whiteboard, your notebook, or digitally – it's up to you. Now, every time you make a decision that saves you money, you make money through the sale of something, or you manage to negotiate yourself a bargain, record the saving against the tangible and/or rewarding thing you want it to go towards. Saved £500 by asking your mate's band to lend you their PA system? Awesome – now allocate it to the family weekend away you always wanted with Grandpa.

## Digital Money Pots

At the time of writing (May 2019), there is something called Monzo. It's a digital bank that we think is pretty cool. You can access the service via an app on your phone, is easy to set up and would be ideal for managing you wedding budget. With Monzo, you can create 'pots' into which you allocate your pennies. Every time you make a saving, say no to bread, or find an artful way around a spot of wedding decor, put the equivalent amount into one of these pots. Before you know it, you'll have saved enough for a load of fun things to do *after* the wedding, meaning the fun can continue beyond the big day.

# CHALLENGING THE NORMS AND BREAKING TRADITIONS

This little nugget has been tucked in straight after finance as we really think this is where you can either A) needlessly dribble away your money or B) save lots of money very easily whilst staying true to what your big day is all about. We are talking about the traditions and 'norms' that seem to surround the idea of what a wedding 'should' be.

A 'Social Norm' is an informal rule that has come to govern behaviour in a group or society; for years, anthropologists and sociologists have been studying how they motivate people to act. Like an informal group of laws, they define what is acceptable and what is not in a group or society. It is not something that has been designed, but that has emerged as a result of humans interacting with one another.

What relevance is this phenomena to weddings? Well for as long as you have been on this planet, you have heard and observed other people planning their weddings and in the process, developed a framework in your head of what a wedding *should* be like. How you should look, what you should wear, who you should invite, what people will be expecting.

Weird isn't it? Why is it that when it comes to weddings, we all somehow feel compelled to do things we feel we *should* do, rather than what we really *want to?*

Cultural traditions undoubtedly have a role to play, but so too does that troublesome human habit of making comparisons. Yes we hear things about other weddings and attend those of our friends and family, but what we are now also exposed to is that wonderful and cursed thing called social media. Back in the day we'd be limited to reading about the Royals in OK magazine, but now fairy tale weddings are everywhere. Companies trying to sell you the dream experience, the dream dress or the most sartorial of suits. In our online bubbles we are fed optimised imagery that is designed exactly for people like us, searching for inspiration and in the process, continually forcing us to make comparisons between our weddings and those of a couple getting wed in an orangery 1500 miles away in California with their two Hungarian Vizslas bearing the wedding rings.

# "Comparison is the thief of joy."
## – Theodore Roosevelt

**Social Norm Alert**: How do you know when you're becoming a victim of a negative social norm? It's when you say stuff like:

- "I guess we probably should invite your friend's girlfriend..."
- "Most couples do a first dance so I guess we should too"
- "All the weddings I've been to give you favours so we should too, right?"

Noticing when you say things like this is super important. It's a big neon sign warning you that you may about to do something you don't want to.

When this happens, think about what value conforming to that norm will add to your wedding day. Will refusing to conform take away any enjoyment or meaning of the day for you? No? Then say 'screw you norms' and shove them back in their norms box.

Our norms will be different to yours of course, but here are a few examples for you to think about.

| Social Norm | Alternative |
|---|---|
| Employ a baker to make your wedding cake | Ask your friend to make it. She loves buns! |
| Provide drinks for everyone | Ask people to bring a bottle for the evening! |
| Have a florist supply your bouquet | Grow your own! |
| Invite everyone whose wedding you were invited to. | Invite your family only. |
| Rustic bread with the main course. | (Rustic?! What does that even mean?!). No bread. |

Pudding can be a particularly easy one to buck the norm with. Firstly, you could always serve your wedding cake as pudding to save it the sad, inevitable 'death by drunken and unappreciative mauling' OR you could ask a few of your very lovely friends to bring a pudding. We did this and we can't tell you how much delight we took in walking up to our pudding BUFFET on our wedding day!

For some more examples of things you can make /do yourself and the kind of money you'll save, see the Annex.

*Victoria genuinely did not know what to do with herself at the sight of so much dessert*

# SIZE MATTERS
# (THE GUEST LIST)

The purported benefits of big over small have been argued about since God created Adam and Eve got a look, but here we are talking guest lists and if you are not careful, they can get BIG! The more your guest list grows, so does the cost (more guests = more mouths to feed, more bums to seat... you get the picture), but cost isn't the only thing that gets affected.

From the moment one said a teary eyed 'yes' to the other, you have probably heard over and over again how quickly your wedding day will go. Let's reiterate that for you - it goes Usain-bloody-Bolt quick. So much so that it almost seems unfair on reflection - all that build up to a day which is over before you know it?!!?

So ask yourself: How many of those precious minutes/hours do you want to spend making small talk with people you invited out of politeness and how much do you want to spend ferociously hugging, singing, dancing and laughing with those you love most?

### Exercise: Tackling the "we probably should's"
This may sound a little brutal but then, deciding who makes the guest list can be just that. This should ideally be done solo first, followed by a get together to see where there are clear agreements and where there might be a need for our good old friend, compromise.

> **Step 1:** Write a full list of all the friends and family you think you want at the wedding
> **Step 2:** Allocate each guest to one of the following categories:

- Must - those closest to your heart, you would be gutted if they couldn't make it/weren't there on the day, the kind of person you would want at your last supper/yearly Christmas dinner.
- Should - you can imagine yourselves happily sharing a drink and a natter with them on the night or someone you would catch up with over a coffee/beer for fun OR to not invite them would cause family upset that you would rather avoid.
- Could - May be a friend or relative's partner not well known to you or a somewhat distant relative[1], but you don't know them well enough to make a call on it right now.

- **Step 3:** Get back together with your partner in crime and compare your lists.
  - 'Musts' on both lists = immediately in.
  - 'Should's' on both lists = make the list but may be subject to discussion depending on total guest numbers.
  - 'Could's' = Depending on numbers, you could discuss adding these guests on to the list with a question mark or add them to an evening guest list.

---

[1] *Caveat:* Sadly, as we grow up, time spent with extended family may get reduced to rare family gatherings such as weddings and funerals. It is therefore worth thinking about how important staying in contact with family is to you. This is not to say that all family should immediately jump to the 'Must' list but do consider trying to arrange a catch up if they don't make the wedding.

## Evening Guest!? Won't they think we're cheap!?

Despite a certain amount of taboo surrounding evening invites, they are actually fairly common these days - there is a growing understanding that weddings aren't cheap! Anyone worth wanting at your wedding would feel stoked to be invited at all rather than 'snubbed'.

## Ebb and flow of friendships

Something you may have already come to realise as you have grown older and wiser is that almost without knowing, some people will phase both in and out of your life. If you look at your wedding list and realise that some people are now in the 'could' or 'should' categories, that isn't a horrible or bad thing. That's life. Some people are meant to be in your life fleetingly, some will stay with you for the entire journey. You'll change, they'll change. It's up to you how you apply this to your guest selection, just don't spend too long agonizing over whether to invite people that seemed to have slipped out the exit door while you weren't looking.

FRIENDSHIPS MOVE ON AND IT'S OK

# GUEST LIST RULES

When it comes down to deciding which of your friends and family to invite, if you are still struggling, it may be handy to have a rule or two in your pocket.

## "Any fool can make a rule
## And any fool will mind it."

– Henry David Thoreau

Why have a rule?
A rule or two can have two beautifully liberating benefits:
1. It helps you be super objective and helps you get to a decision quicker.
2. If you ever find yourself having to explain why someone didn't make the cut, it sounds far less personal to say you had a rule you agreed to stick to and sadly that person didn't meet it.

Examples of a guest list rule might include "both of us have to have met them", or "we must have seen them in the last year / two years".

### Caveat 1:
First things first - you don't have to create rules. If you are truly happy having both big fat family fern trees there, you crack right on. Secondly, if you are also happy tackling the omission of certain relatives and/or their partners head on without feeling the need for explanation then more power to you!

## Caveat 2:

If there is someone who you both agree is worth breaking the rule for (ours was a great aunt and uncle that Kara hadn't met yet) then do just that! Your wedding, your rules. If you are particularly guilt prone / awkward at the thought of breaking said rule, get that person round for dinner or lined up for a coffee date asap and TA DAAA - they've made the cut.

# RULES CAN SET YOU FREE

# MANAGING PARENTS

After some very rigorous research (multiple barbecues and beers over the course of several years) we discovered some fascinating insights about how differently people's parents react to the whole wedding thing. You only need to watch 20 seconds of 'Say Yes to the Dress' or 'Here comes the Bride' to conduct your own research and come to the conclusion that sometimes this can be very tricky!

There is no magic silver bullet for marital bliss, and you know your parents and the complexities of your family's dynamics better than us, but here are two tips to think about when bringing your folks into the process:

## Tip 1: Avoid cash chat (By Kara)

In some circles, families of the betrothed want to contribute to the wedding. Before my father had even hit the 'send' button on a bank transfer he said 'chook, the only proviso is that you don't discuss the amount with anyone'. Now this may sound a little Godfather/Sopranos-esque to you and although my dad is quite the party hound, he's no drug lord and is actually turning out to be rather sensible in his old age. What Dad was protecting against was this: even in the most loving of families, parents can feel like money contributed = love shown. This can have the unintended effect of either putting parents under pressure to contribute more than they can afford and /or making those that have contributed less money feel inadequate.

So by all means, gratefully accept that parental wedding investment (just check if there are any T&Cs), hug them and let them know how grateful you are (for whatever amount it may be) then say no more. To anyone.

Tip 2: Share the fun

In the 'traditional' wedding setup there is usually a distinctive role for the father of the bride but not a whole lot required of the other parents. Some parents may be quite happy with this and enjoy the stress-free task of simply sharing the day with you. However, there is also the risk that some parents may feel slightly left out or 'forgotten' in amongst all the tradition.

The only way of knowing? Have the chat! Ask your parents if they would like to be involved in the day and / or build up to the wedding in any way. Don't feel you have to follow tradition and consider having parents do non-traditional roles such as giving readings, walk you down the aisle (who says it can't be your mum *and* dad?) or even give a speech. Just don't be offended if they say no - weddings, after all, can be hard work and after many years of raising you, they've earnt their right to sit back and enjoy.

# GRATITUDE

Whoever we are, whatever we are doing, wherever we now find ourselves, we have something to be grateful for. It may be our health, our friends, the birdsong, the blue sky above. Now and again, if you just stop for one moment, put your hand on your heart, and just think about all those things you are grateful for, those things that you've been blessed to have done, experienced, and felt, you'll fill your mind and body with nothing but positive energy. You'll no longer complain about the service at that café on the corner – you'll appreciate how lucky you are to be able to do this – to have coffee with a friend whenever you like. You won't complain that you can't play football anymore because of that injury you had, you'll be thankful for all those years of camaraderie and friendship and the opportunity now to do something new.

The power of gratitude is that it empowers you to recognise the things that people do for you, the kindness they have shown you, the love they have for you. We don't do it enough, especially for our parents. As a bare minimum, they brought you into the world, but the truth is, they've probably made a heap load of sacrifices for you and you're likely their proudest life's work.

Whatever or however they wish to contribute, be thankful. Fill your heart with gratitude and love for them and tell them what they mean to you.

This is really something you should do anyway, whether you're getting married or not. Seriously, go tell them now.

Life's too short.

# LOCATION, LOCATION

When it comes to finding the venue, two things need to be at play here, people: your heart AND your head.

What do we mean by that?

If you are someone that leads with your heart, you may visit a venue and instantly say "I love it, it's perfect!" If you're the type that leads with your head, you may be a little more practical, saying stuff like, "it has no accommodation on site", or "it's a bit outside our budget".

Yes, it's tempting to call our 'Thinker' partner 'boring' or 'Feeling' partner a 'dreamer' or 'impractical', but your wedding has to work for you from an emotional perspective AND hit the budget, so both mind-sets are equally indispensable when it comes down to venue selection.

Why? Good decisions are not based purely on emotions, but on rationality and sound judgement, something we can't do without engaging our grey matter. You want to be sure your venue:
- Is within budget
- Helps you hit your priorities
- Doesn't contain restrictions that would ruin your enjoyment of the day (e.g. early curfew, not enough space)

A certain amount of heart and gut feel goes a long way and if a place hits those vital spots for the both of you (i.e. you can both envisage getting married there and it feels exciting to do so), you are probably on to a winner. Just don't dive in without being a little bit boring and thinking about the practicalities of things.

*Before starting the venue hunt,* consider writing out a quick list – those things that your heads think are important, and those things your hearts feel are important. To help you along, we've put a few prompts in the Annex for you to think about.

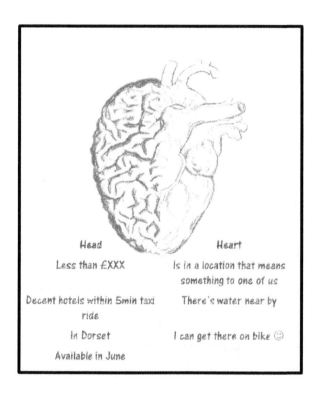

| Head | Heart |
|---|---|
| Less than £XXX | Is in a location that means something to one of us |
| Decent hotels within 5min taxi ride | There's water near by |
| In Dorset | I can get there on bike ☺ |
| Available in June | |

Speaking from experience... we rushed in and nailed all practical priorities in our first venue choice (no corkage fees *tick*, open field with loads of dancing space *tick* people could camp for free if they wanted *tick*). But when that fell through and we were starting again, Will, in one of his beautifully profound moments, said:

"We thought about what we wanted, but we didn't necessarily think about where we wanted it and most importantly, why?"

End result: we went from a field in the countryside with no connection to us to a lovely spot on the Dorset coastline. Will got his seaside dream (Pisces through and through), I got my beloved Purbecks. TICK, TICK - BOOM!

*A few extra tips:*

- Stay open minded - it is amazing what filling a room with some lights, flowers and happy people can do to a space.

- Even if the venue itself doesn't have many photos for inspiration, quite often simply typing in the venue name + 'wedding' to a google search leads to professional photographer's pages popping up with photos from when they covered weddings there. Having a flick through their photos can provide you with lots of ideas on what is possible and how different couples put their own mark on the place. Do this only if you are stuck though and not too fussed about the creative process – otherwise you'll be anchored to what's been done before and you'll miss out on coming up with your own ideas ☺.

- Don't spend too much time worrying about where people will find accommodation. Yes, it is good to think about ensuring immediate family could stay nearby (or onsite) and yes, it is a massive bonus if you have somewhere nearby for grooms/bridal parties to get ready but outside of that, it's not your problem. If people really want to be there, they'll find a way to ensure they can make it.

# NOM NOM

The discussion of all things gourmet is tactically placed right after venue selection as food quite often features fairly high on people's priority list for their wedding day. You can of course ask everyone to bring a picnic to a park, but if you're thinking about catering for your guests, here are some pointers - the amount, type and timing of your food can all play a role in shaping not only how the day runs, but how your guests feel through the day.

## Put yourself in their shoes

There is a surprisingly simple relationship that exists between the happiness of your guests and the amount of food they have eaten.

1.  Not enough food = hungry, grumpy & possibly quite piddled guests.
2.  Too much food = full, tired, "not sure I can even contemplate the dancefloor" guests.

This relationship is shown graphically overleaf.

# A Graphical Representation Of The Relationship Between Guest Happiness and Quantity Eaten

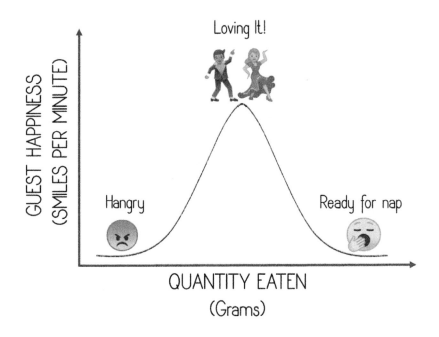

For those unfamiliar with the term, 'Hangry', as per our diagram, is when you are so hungry you can't help but be an arse, becoming snappy and irrational ("NO I DON'T WANT CRISPS, I WANT FOOD!!"). It's a serious medical condition that can only be overcome with food of the sufferer's desire.

When it comes to dealing with someone suffering from this condition, our advice would be to avoid completely, unless their desired foodstuff is in your possession. If feeding the sufferer by hand, keep your thumbs in. Like you are feeding a horse.

*Above: Richard Westall's Sword of Damocles, 1812*

*Research suggests that the origins of the Sword of Damocles are actually rooted not in "an allusion to the imminent and ever-present peril faced by those in positions of power", but "an allusion to the imminent and ever-present fear of the onset of Hangriness in one's partner at a public event like a wedding".*

## Cuisine

What you eat and how you eat it is a core consideration as it can set the tone for the entire day. If you are envisaging something formal, then a sit down affair to some traditional dishes may be just the ticket. If however, you want more of a party/relaxed vibe, then street food vans can allow people to mingle easily and not feel confined to their chairs. Just choose a good MC to make sure the speeches aren't missed!

## Exercise: World Culinary Tour

With a view to enjoying the process, write down a list of all the cuisines you fancy exploring. Think that some dim sum might be awesome? Write it down. Think that some Fish and Chips could be the ticket? Write it down. Now, book one meal a month, or week, to try it out – it could be a meal out or you could make it yourself. This is the perfect opportunity to travel the world from the safety of your own dining room table. What better reason to experiment than to be informing your own wedding menu?!

## Timing

Be mindful not to leave your wedding guests waiting too long for food... particularly if there are only canapes on offer when the bar has opened.

*Welcome drinks + empty stomach = high risk of peaking too soon*

It is even worth mentioning when food will be served on invites (or on an 'additional info' sheet) to allow guests to prepare appropriately.

One more thing! We love our food, but if we, or indeed anyone is sat on their arse for 5 hours with an increasingly bloated stomach, they'll generally get rather bored (or in Will's case, narcoleptic). Don't be afraid to get your guests moving to keep the excitement alive! Play games or have one of the courses standing up and consider getting your guests to self-serve. It is an excuse for people to move and mingle and may even save you some money (less waiting staff required).

## Choosing your caterers

- Ask for recommendations. Just like David Gandy posing in his Dolce Gabbana undies, a caterer's Instagram shot of their tender loins doesn't actually mean they are all that tasty (sorry David, I'm sure you taste delicious!). The only way to know if a caterer can produce great food really is word of mouth.

- DIY. Depending on the size of your guest list, setting out to do your own wedding catering is nothing short of bloody bonkers (you will either be taking on far too much or end up palming serving duties off on your family members) BUT there is no reason why you can't save money and put a personal touch on the day by providing at least some of the food. Just keep in mind the logistics of heating and serving food and whether it is worth the hassle if your caterers aren't happy to do this for you.

- Think outside the wedding caterer - if you have a favourite restaurant or cafe you visit regularly, it is always worth asking if they ever do catering or would consider catering for your big day.

## Make sure *YOU* eat

It may sound like we are mothering you here but you really do need to remember to take time to eat. Your wedding day is one big, euphoric love fest and a common regret among couples is that they got so caught up in it all that they never really got to enjoy their wedding food. So when dinner comes out, sit your newlywed butt down and try at least 5 minutes of some mindful eating.

Mmmmmmm.

# CHOOSING YOUR OUTFIT

**From Kara's perspective:**

Being far from the next Gok Wan, I will admit to knowing very little about fashion. My idea of an outstanding outfit mostly centres around lycra and elasticated waist bands - a comfort-first approach. So rather than pretend I know my 'A line's' from my 'Empires', I will be sharing two tips and one consoling insight from a friend that completely changed my attitude to finding the dress of your dreams - 'the one'.

## Tip one: Make a day of it

I have an admission that may physically repulse some women but .... I really don't like shopping. I do, however, have quite the penchant for food and prosecco. So my approach to wedding dress shopping was to treat it as a day out - invite a few friends (ideally mix those that haven't yet met - great way to fast forward Hen Do introductions), get slightly piddled on free prosecco then soak it up over a chat and lunch.
With all the attention, lots of beautiful dresses, and copious amounts of ladies cooing about how *"gooorgeous"* I looked, I ended up actually rather enjoying myself. Did I mention I love prosecco?

## Tip two: Pre-Loved

Although I visited lots of lovely shops and tried on lots of beautiful dresses, I never actually intended on buying a wedding dress full price. I really hope this doesn't put me on some sort of wedding shop blacklist, but the dresses I loved by the designers I loved were way out of our price range and I needed to find a work around. Winning some cash on the lottery that I never enter was fairly unlikely, so searching the pre-loved websites was a key strategy I utilised (in the end I was lucky enough to find a sample dress that won the race to first place so the wedding dress shops had their uses!).

The benefits of buying second hand don't, however, merely start and end with just saving you £££'s. You see, when indulging in a (now rare) 'night out' I never quite seem to make it to the finish line without somehow indulging my outfit in at least one food or drink stain to mark the evening and as we were intending for our wedding to be one epic party, I needed to be prepared for my dress to wear the war wounds of a great night out. By buying my dress as a sample, we not only saved money, we also saved the stress of worrying if something happened to it on the day. I adored my dress but I also dragged it through pine needles, dropped to my knees throwing sweaty air guitars and ran round with sparklers like a 4 year old in it and not once did I worry 'is my dress ok?' That freedom is priceless if you ask me ☺.

## The consoling shared insight

I think I was up to wedding dress shop number four when, despite still having a surprisingly awesome time, I couldn't help but feel a little underwhelmed... Why wasn't I getting that 'oh my word I look bloody GORGEOUS'/Gwyneth - getting-her-Oscar kind of reaction? Was I dead from the tear ducts down? Officially immune to feeling wowed by me in a wedding dress? Voicing this slight concern to my friend Tatiana she said "Kara, I never had that moment either. I just chose the dress I liked the most".

Now I don't mean to downplay the dress experience here ladies - I can assure you that once I chose my dress and had it fitted to me, my mum cried. Once I put it on for my wedding day . . . well, I still didn't cry but I did finally feel like a beautiful blushing bride. So please don't let this dampen your excitement but do be mindful of Tatiana's advice and lower the expectation of being utterly blown away when you slip on 'the' dress for the first time.

If I had one piece of advice to you, it would be this: Find a dress or outfit that makes you *feel* beautiful and be confident that the smile, love and excitement that you'll radiate on the day will make it something amazing.

From Will's perspective:

I thought I would find myself an outfit in a weekend. I didn't. I think I may have gone to more suit shops than Kara. This is what I learnt and this is my advice to you.

Style is personal.
My style is not your style.
Yours is not your friends'.
It's not what you wear, it's how you wear it.
Wear clothes that you will feel good in, that reflect all your wonderful idiosyncrasies.
Love your style and own it.
Different colour shoes?
All colours look the same in Grayscale.

"I BUY EXPENSIVE SUITS. THEY JUST LOOK CHEAP ON ME."

– Warren Buffet

# YOU'LL FIND ME AT THE BAR (DRINKS)

People need hydrating. How you wish to achieve this goal is 100% up to you. At the bare minimum, there should be water and whilst your guests could queue up and use their hands to drink from a single tap or handpump, there should ideally also be some drinking vessels like Mammoth tusks, upturned skulls from your ancestors or what are now known as 'cups'.

Anything that you wish to provide beyond that is up to you and your budget, but above all, your approach to the running of the wedding bar should be reflective of your attitudes to drinking.

Tee total or not big drinkers yourselves? Then it probably follows that you won't be too worried about the role of alcohol in the day. If people want to drink more than you've allowed for, point them towards the bar. Indeed, if alcohol doesn't fit into your life, who says you have to have alcohol there at all?

On the other hand, if you enjoy a tipple and consider alcohol an important aspect of the day, then you do need to think a little more about the provision and cost of alcohol as decisions made early on may really impact your wallet!

**How much alcohol will we need?**

If you're doing the bar yourself and you're anything like me, (Will) I was pretty nervous about running out of alcohol. The thought of thirsty guests and an empty bar sent a shiver down me and I knew nothing about catering for large numbers. I used online calculators as a guide for how much alcohol we were likely to need and quizzed our caterers and wine providers (tap into the knowledge of those that have way more experience than you). I then created a simple little spreadsheet summarising what drinks were needed at which point in the day. I can't emphasise enough that talking to others is really important, so ask the dumb questions as the experts will always have a work around.

When calculating quantities, take into consideration the likely 'thirstiness' of your guests, but also think about how many tea-totallers or pregnant ladies you might have - they'll not be quaffing wine, but they'll certainly get bored of orange juice after 5 hours, so think about some variety when it comes to soft drinks (a simple mocktail perhaps?).

You can find lots of spreadsheets and calculators online, but here's ours as an example - We wrote this plan for each part of the day and then shared it with our caterers, so they knew what to provide our guests and when.

## Wedding Drinks

| Welcome Drinks | | | | | |
|---|---|---|---|---|---|
| Drink | | Stock | Recipe | Notes | Fridge? |
| Hugos | Mint | | 1 Sprig per glass | | |
| | Lagioiosa Prosecco | 20 | 750ml | Recipe Gives 10 | CHILL |
| | Soda Water | 8 | 125ml | champagne | CHILL |
| | Elderflower | 10 | 375ml | glasses | CHILL |
| | | | | | |
| Prosecco | Rivamonte | 12 | | | CHILL |
| | | | | | |
| Beer | Ales (pints) | 100 | | | |
| | Leffe (Keg) | 24 | | | CHILL |
| | Duval (Bottles) | 24 | | | CHILL |
| | Amstel (Bottles) | 196 | | | CHILL |
| | Picon (for lager) | 1 | | | |
| | | | | | |
| Soft Drinks | Orange Juice (Cartons) | 10 | | | |
| | Lemon Squash (Bottles) | 2 | | | |
| | Water | | | | |

## The Corkage Conundrum

How you would like to manage alcohol on the day should be an early discussion between you and the other half, particularly prior to agreeing your venue. Some venues will provide the entire package, give you a price and with some negotiation, you find (or haggle) your way to an agreement. However, if you intend on providing your *own* alcohol, be savvy and ask about corkage (a set amount that they will charge you for every bottle or even glass of alcohol you provide). Some venues don't charge, but if yours does, be 100% clear on how it works, get it written into your contract and write it into your budget. Arguing after anything has been signed is painful and should be avoided.

## Saving Pennies on the DIY Bar

Consider asking guests to 'Bring a bottle' for later on in the evening. Most people will be more than happy to bring their own bottle of spirit to party on to the wee hours with if it saves them the cost of an expensive hotel bar.

You could always brew your own, but we will not provide any further support to how you go about doing this. Whilst we encourage experimentation in every aspect of your life, we do not want to be held accountable for the possible mayhem / personal injury that might ensue.

If you're reading this and live in the UK, you should seriously consider a trip to France for a classy booze cruise. Some of the wine supermarkets will pay for your Euro Tunnel ticket, giving you 24hrs to get to France, pick up your very cost-effective delicious plonk, have an evening in a little chateau, and return the following day. It may only be 24 hours but it is definitely enough to feel you've had a mini break with the added win of saving your bar bill to boot! If it's summer, we'd suggest popping to Le Touquet - sand, sea and very lovely eateries. Big W&K love for Le Touquet.

"Free bar? You're nuts mate"

## Welcome drinks

Choose a welcome drink that is personal to you but also doesn't blow the budget. If you're confused as to why us Brits are obsessed with under-whelming warm Fruit Salad and Mint drizzled with flat lemonade and Pimms, don't have it. There are loads of lovely, often non-alcoholic recipes out there that you can use. Are your welcome drinks being provided by a caterer? Ask them for some alternative ideas - don't just automatically accept their default suggestions.

To help you out with this task, here are a few exercises.

## Exercise: The welcome drink mixology challenge

This can be done as a couple or as a fun dinner party idea with friends.
Set a maximum cost of the drink (e.g. £0.50 per glass)
Each 'player' must either design or select a cocktail of choice to be prepared on the evening.
Each player presents their cocktail to the group and gives a winning pitch on why they think this should be the welcome drink of choice for your wedding. They must also, of course, state the cost of the drink per glass.
You and your partner must then discuss the contenders and make your deciding vote. Consider presenting said friend with a fun prize or naming the drink after them on the wedding day.

Note: This applies for both alcoholic and non-alcoholic drinks / mocktails. Never tried Cranberry Juice and Ginger Ale? Oh you've never lived!

"Mum, we LOVE the way you're thinking, but just how practical do you think that is for 90 people?"

## Exercise: The welcome drink mixology mashup

You repeat the above as a dinner party idea but ask each attendee to bring a spirit of choice. Ensure you have lots of mixers available and challenge each person to create a cocktail with what's available on the night. We suggest all mixing is done in the kitchen for obvious reasons.

**Final Top Tip:**

Consider having a little bottle of something special for you and your partner to share. During the night, sneak off to the bar together to take a sip of your favourite aperitif (ours was Menthe Pastille). Catch up on awesome bits of the day so far, laugh, snog like lusty teenagers then go take the bottle on a tour to continue the party with your guests.

Dear Mr Giffard *et al*, we really hope you don't mind us advertising your drink. It's just so good we don't think it's fair not to tell others about it.

# ENTERTAINMENT: ALL ABOARD THE FUNBUS!

This chapter wasn't put to paper to debate the pros and cons of DJ Vs band or violin duo Vs operatic waiters. That's all a matter of personal taste and is therefore not a topic for guidance or advice. Instead, this fun little foray has two main aims: to save you money and to maximise the enjoyment of the day by all guests (you included).

How?

Do stuff that's free and play games that get all of your guests involved. Here are some ideas:

## The DIY Photo booth

These things come in at a couple of hundred a pop, easily. That's crazy! How about you make your own? All you need is a camera, some fancy dress items and someone willing to spend no more than an hour giving people a count down between pics – it's a wicked way to get people socialising too. If you have an outside venue, put all your kit in a wheel barrow and wheel it between groups. So much fun. If it gets out of hand here and there, so be it. All stories to tell for the day after!

## The Mrs and Mrs Game (French Version)

Get a line-up of 8-12 enthusiastic and banterlicious guests (1 from each table). Read a very short story about the couple, interjected with relevant items (e.g. tissue, lipstick, glasses). On announcing the item, players have to race off into the crowd, get that item off a guest and return to their chair. Last one back on their chair is out. The person who is knocked out is then asked to give the happy couple a gift at some point in the next 12 months, that necessitates the contestant spend some time with the couple. E.g. they must make them dinner, or a chocolate cake, or take then out for a walk one day. It's a lovely way of keeping the connection and celebration going into the next year.
Repeat until only one contestant remains, at which point they may be given a small prize whereby the Bride and Groom do something for them in the next year.

This game has significant potential for carnage as guests rush to and fro, but it's hilarious and very much worth it.

## Go Retro

Remember those playground games (not the ones behind the bike sheds)? Bring them to life - they were enough to entertain us as kids and we dare say that they are more than enough to entertain us now. Treasure hunts, Pin the Tail on the donkey, egg and spoon race, hop scotch - with a bit of thinking you can rejuvenate and adultify these to give you and your guests more than enough entertainment. We also bet that if you were to task up a few of your friends to organise these games for you, they'll be more inventive than you could ever imagine. Just give them a time slot and some other constraints if needed, and ask them to keep it a surprise until the day. It's another job off your list and another surprise to look forward to come the big day.

# THE CEREMONY

Whether you are having it in a church, hotel field, underwater or skydiving, here are a few tips on the wedding ceremony that we would like to share.

## Make it personal

Although writing our own 'promises'/vows to each meant we were both dabbing away at our lovesick tears during that part of the ceremony (yep, it catches you out, people!), there is a lot to be said for personalising or even writing your own vows. Even if it is a few lines, having something that you know your partner has taken the time to sit, think about and put pen to paper for means a lot more than just following a script. You don't have to be the next Shakespeare, just keep it simple and speak from the heart. Oh, and don't share them with each other before the wedding if you can help it, although it's useful to agree how many lines you are going to say so that it's not massively one-sided.

## Readings

If you are asking people to read something at your ceremony, keep it a surprise! It's awesome to think that that person has taken the time to find something or even write something for you both to share in that moment.

## Memories

Although at the time you will feel like you are soaking it up and will never forget a word uttered from your loved one's adoring lips, reality is that you will. You'll actually forget quite a lot of it. Just like you take pictures to help you capture moments, consider making an album where you collect in both the vows, the ceremony script and any readings done. Being able to read back over the day not only brings back lovely memories but can remind you of the promises you made to each other.

"Of course I remember your vows ... What were they again?"

# THE BUILD UP

In the last few days and weeks leading up to your big day, you will likely have several opportunities for moments of joy, but may also feel some anxiety and tension.

Why?

Because you care. You will have loved ones arriving from potentially all over the country or even the globe. You will feel a certain amount of responsibility to spend time with said loved ones but at the same time you have a seemingly growing list of things to get done. How your wedding build up story pans out depends on two very important things:

## 1. Perspective
## 2. Organisation

### Getting organised

Have a task list ready to go and ideally discuss delegation of jobs ahead of time so that everyone knows what they are doing in the days leading up to the wedding. Give people as much warning as possible that they will be expected to help too - this will help with their planning and if it involves anything they might not have done before, it will allow them to mentally prepare. For example, if you're asking them to be an MC, it will allow them to get some material together to pad out the quiet bits.

Ensure people have all the equipment required to carry out their tasks in one place - this can reduce the multiple questions on pre-wed day when only you and your partner know the location of suddenly 'critical' items (note: buy more than 1 pair of scissors!).

*Know your limits!* Don't commit to going for full-on 5 star hosting. Yes, of course you may want to open your home up to people but don't also feel like you have to be preparing meals or copious amounts of tea and coffee for everyone. Get a tea and coffee stand easily accessible for all to self-serve their hot beverages. Make sure there are cold beers and lots of milk in the fridge. Get everyone to chuck in £10 and order in take-out or see if your local café could cater (you can also order trays of sandwiches/wraps and large salads etc. from your local bakery or food store). You never know, you may even be lucky enough to have a family member that loves cooking and is happy to do the cheffing for you. Do not be afraid to ask friends for help.

## Maintaining perspective

Lots of little jobs can lead to lots of narrowing of the wed-crazed mind. It is easy to forget how precious this time is when you can't remember where you put the superglue or who has the seating plan. We aren't saying you can just "Namaste" this one out and forget the To-Do list but don't let it engulf and overwhelm the entire experience either. You never know when you will get the opportunity to have all these people in one place again.

So by all means, get your jobs done, crack on and delegate where needed but also take the time for a relaxing celebratory dinner or sneak in a cup of tea/afternoon beer with your friend from afar in amongst the chaos. These precious moments will be over before you know it.

# THE BIG DAY

This is it!!!

You've arrived!

Whatever hasn't been done now, isn't going to get done, so back yourself that you've delegated all required tasks and stick any niggling worries in a big beautiful balloon and …. Let go!

There are no tips needed here - you are about to share one of the best days of your life with all your favourite people. Stand, breathe and fill yourself with gratitude.

You know when people say take a moment, just the two of you, to stand back on the outskirts of your wedding and peer on in? To relish the glow of warm fuzzy love that hits your heart as you watch all those people dance, drink and laugh together because they want to be part of celebrating YOU? Do that. It's awesome.

# ~ANNEX~

## WEDMIN-SMASHING TOOLS

Throughout this book, we've mentioned some tools, referenced some people and talked about things you could read. Here's a list of all those things. If there is something we've missed, please let us know.

### Tools for managing tasks
- o Trello for Digital To-Do Lists (www.trello.com)
- o Sticky notes / Post-Its for to-do lists (www.post-it.com)
- o Google Sheets for Spreadsheets (https://www.google.com/sheets/about)

### Tools to help with Creative Stuff
- o Use Apps like Prisma to convert boring pictures into amazing art works for invites. www.prismaai.com
- o Adobe Spark (www.spark.adobe.com/)
- o Canva (www.canva.com/)
- o www.fiverr.com for people to help you make your invites
- Online inspiration (Beware – comparison is the death of joy)
  - o Pinterest (www.pinterest.com)
  - o Instagram (www.instagram.com)
- Offline inspiration (the best)
  - o Go to a gallery, a sculpture park, a vinyl record store, your local Arts University, your creative friend's house, your local library, wherever you are never, and voraciously consume the random

stuff. It's through this consumption of stuff that you connect the dots and create the awesome.

## Where to buy, hire or sell second hand wedding gear:
- Gumtree (www.gumtree.com)
- Preloved (www.preloved.com)
- Sell my Wedding (www.sellmywedding.com)
- www.bride2bride.co.uk
- www.preloved.com
- www.gumtree.com
- www.oxfam.org.uk/shop/bridal/wedding-dresses

## Tools to help with budget management
- Monzo (www.monzo.com)
- Money Supermarket (www.moneysupermarket.com)

## Places to create a free personalised website for your wedding ((People WILL lose your invite and ask you for the details again)
- www.gettingmarried.co.uk
- www.wix.com
- www.wordpress.org
- www.facebook.com

## Personality tests to find out more about each other:
- http://www.humanmetrics.com/cgi-win/jtypes2.asp

## Some other brain candy that we love:
- https://austinkleon.com/
- Books:

- o  It's Not How Good You Are, It's How Good You Want To Be. Arden, Paul. 2003
- o  Whatever You Think, Think Opposite. Arden, Paul. 2006
- o  Steal Like an Artist. Kleon, Austin. 2012
- http://www.thesartorialist.com/
- Paper or plastic? How disposable bag bans, fees and taxes affect consumer behaviour. Homonoff, T, 2017. https://theconversation.com/paper-or-plastic-how-disposable-bag-bans-fees-and-taxes-affect-consumer-behavior-48858.

## Moscow Mule

*Ingredients*

1.5floz Vodka

0.5floz Fresh Lime Juice

0.5 Cup Ginger Beer (the more fiery the better)

1 lime wedge

Handful of Ice

*Method*

Put ice in a tall tumbler or copper mug if you have one. Pour vodka, lime juice and ginger beer over the ice. Stir slowly to combine ingredients. Drop in the lime wedge for show and enjoy.

# LITTLE WAYS TO SAVE PENNIES – A FEW EXAMPLES

| ...Vs... | | = approximate cost saving |
|---|---|---|
| Chiller Van | Cool boxes or wheelbarrows full of ice | £300-400 |
| Florist-made table flowers | Bulk ordering a bucket of flowers to arrange yourself or opt for something non-flower related (think books, bottles, candles, balloons) | £100-300 |
| Real flower bouquets for bridesmaids | Faux flowers or even beautifully decorated lanterns which your bridesmaids can keep forever. | £50-200 |
| Linen napkins | Paper napkins | £100-140 |
| Musicians playing music for your ceremony | Asking your friend to hit 'play' on a Spotify playlist | £200-800 |
| Professional wedding cake | Asking a friend/(s) to make you a cake or cupcakes | £200-500 |
| Wedding favours (e.g. mini bottles of alcohol or sweets) | Forget the favours. No one misses them! | £100-300 |

| | | |
|---|---|---|
| Professionally designed and printed save the date cards (+ postage) | Keep it simple with e-mails/online messages (but go old school and send a letter if the "off the grid" folks are likely to miss this!) | £100-200 |
| Professionally designed and printed wedding invites (+ postage) | Design yourself (or steal ideas from online) then print at home or get quotes from local printing companies. Printing in black and white can save you even more ££££ (also don't forget to get a sample before you do the whole lot! ) | £100-200 |
| Champagne for speeches/toasts | Swap to champagne's more cost effective but lovely sisters (e.g. prosecco, cava) Or skip the extra cost – just ask them to raise the glass they have already! | £100-400 |

# VENUE CONSIDERATIONS

Some things to think about when visiting your venues:

- Overall cost (and are there cheaper alternatives? E.g. getting married on a Friday or out of season)
- Hidden costs (e.g. toilet hire, generator hire)
- Deposit required (before you pay one - check the T&Cs!)
- Cut off time for music
- Set up time beforehand and kick out time the next day
- Is there enough shelter for people or will you have to hire marquees?
- Accommodation options - can people stay on site or if not, are there hotels/B&Bs/camp sites nearby?
- Distance to ceremony venue (if separate to your reception venue)
- Do they allow food to be brought in or is all catering in house? If in house, what are the costs?
- Can you bring your own alcohol in or will there be a corkage fee?
- How many guests can the venue fit?
- What does your *head* say?
- What does your *heart* say?

# ABOUT THE AUTHORS...

A few days after I started "Wedmin Like a Boss" (the original title of this book), I shared the idea with my wife Kara and since that point we've built it together. It's been wicked fun and by applying both our very diverse toolkits to the challenge of Wedmin, we think we've created something awesome - a pocket guide that will give you a few helpful nudges to help you think about how you go about envisioning and enjoying one of the most memorable days of your life (so far). It takes into account all the lessons we learnt about wedding planning, but also those we've collated from friends and family in our research. We've then taken all those lessons and applied our skills and experience in our day jobs to give you some useful tools and techniques to help you along your way. I work a lot with people, developing ideas and building stuff. Kara is a lecturer, with skills in understanding how people tick and what motivates them. She is also, painfully, funnier and way more straight-talking than I am, which is useful when we are writing together.

When talking about the idea for the book to my Mum, she was reading The Times and said that they did this cool section sometimes called 'How We Met', where couples would describe how they came to be. We thought that would be pretty good fun to do and interesting for you to learn about the folk whose book you've just read. So here it goes.

# ...AND HOW WE MET

## Kara's Version

I'm afraid I won't be Mills and Boon romancing you with a story about love at first sight - it's hard to fall heart-wrenchingly in love with someone when they are stood on a rugby pitch shouting at themselves, wearing an intriguing combination of brightly coloured board shorts, rugby socks and a camouflage thermal top. Our friend Snow summed it up perfectly when she said "Will, you look like a 4 year old that's been allowed to dress himself". But in a slow cooker pot of intrigue, flirting and finally, love, I slowly learnt that Will's self-directed shouting on the pitch had little resemblance to his true character.... In fact, it was far from it and once the sweaty, multi-patterned outer layer was removed, underneath was something truly incredible.

How did we get there? It was actually his adorably awful chat up line (delivered in an equally adorable Welsh accent) that sealed him his first drunken kiss with me. But the falling in love bit? Well that came from much more. It was watching his kindness and generosity with complete strangers, admiring his contagious enthusiasm for creativity and adventure, and laughing with him at, well, almost anything. I hope if you are reading this book, you have peeled back the layers of your own 'Will' and found qualities in him/her that inspire you, create little bubbles of admiration and love in you and make you stand back every now and then and just go 'wow, I am one lucky human'. If all that sounds familiar then: massive congrats on finding a premium quality life partner champ!)

## Will's Version

Our friend Snow did indeed say that about my attire, but whilst I agree, I'd say that I was more like a 4yr old who has been allowed to dress himself *in the dark*. Regarding my side of the 'how we met' story, it was Kara's beaming smile, amazing bottom and her passion for people, fun and indeed rugby that really caught my eye. Wherever she was, she'd be radiating a fiery energy like no-one else I had ever met and a sense of humour that could only have been developed in Australia, a country I would later learn is completely devoid of social boundaries. After a few months of rugby pitch banter, it was on a trip up

100

North that I decided to make my move. Sat in the back of the minibus listening to Kara finding herself hilarious, I carefully developed a fool-proof strategy and locked it away for later execution. After a day of rugby, we were 'out, out', in a nightclub when I saw my chance. I strode confidently across the room, leaving the team kitty (money, not cat) on a ping pong table, and held her firmly by the midriff. After no doubt some weapon grade A Class preamble, wit and repartee, I gave her both barrels, the *crème da la crème* of chat up lines. The motherlode. Looking into her eyes I said "I find you very sexually attractive". The poor girl had no chance. Four years on, happily married and writing this book, I know I have utterly lucked out. She's turbo awesome and I am blessed to have her in my life.

# THANK YOU

Without these wonderful, brilliant people, our book would have been tinier and not half as fun to write. Thank you...

Padre Tom for all your wisdom.

Ele, Ali and Mummy Roberts for your proof reading and feedback.

Keita for coming to Europe and giving us a deadline by which to write this book.

All our inspirational friends for their insights, ideas and creativity (you know who you are).

Paul Arden, Austin Kleon, Seth Godin, Tony Robbins, Ann Lamott and all those folk we'll likely never meet but who continue to inspire us with their ruckus making.

All the people who dreamt up the inspiring words we quoted.

To Victoria, Aunty Steph, Tom (with Wheelbarrow on head) and Chris for letting us use their images.

The brilliant Tom Huntington, with whom Will first set a goal as part of MyCharter.me to get something written and out there.

And last but not least, You, the reader, for spending your hard earned pennies on our little book - it's been so much fun to write and we hope you enjoyed it.

ISBN: 9781086014181

First Published in 2019 by W&K Creative Ltd

Version 2.0 Published 22/09/2019

Text © 2019 W&K Creative Ltd

Imagery © 2019 W&K Creative Ltd

Printed in Great Britain
by Amazon